SO-AEE-995

Ann O. Squire

Spiders of North America

Franklin Watts - A Division of Grolier Publishing
New York • London • Hong Kong • Sydney • Danbury, Connecticut

Photographs ©: Animals Animals 39 (J A L. Cooke/OSF), 7 (M. Fogdem/OSF), 36, 37 (Joe McDonald), 20, 21 (Bertram G Murray, Jr.); Dwight R. Kuhn Photography: 22, 23, 25; Joe Warfel: 14, 15; NHPA: 18, 19 (G. J. Cambridge), 27 (Stephen Dalton); Photo Researchers: 17 (Alan L. Detrick), 5 bottom left (Andrew J. Martinez), 13 (Stephen P. Parker), 33 (Dr. Paul A. Zahi); Visuals Unlimited: 30, 31 (Bill Beatty), 35 (Cheryl A. Ertelt), 5 top left (Greg Gorel), cover (Jeffley Howe), 41 (Robert Lindholm), 5 top right (Ken Lucas), 5 bottom right (Glenn Oliver), 29 (Doug Sokell); Wildlife Collection: 6 (Gene Boaz), 42 (Chris Huss), 1 (Charles Melton), 43 (John Tyson), 40 (Tom Vezo).

Illustrations by Jose Gonzales and Steve Savage

Visit Franklin Watts on the Internet at:
http://publishing.grolier.com

Library of Congress Cataloging-in-Publication Data

Squire, Ann O.
Spiders of North America / Ann O. Squire.
        p. cm. — (Animals in order)
    Includes bibliographical references and index.
    Summary: Describes the physical characteristics and behavior of a variety of North American spiders, including spiders in fields, gardens, around the house, underground, and in the water.
    ISBN 0-531-11516-X (lib. bdg.)   0-531-16449-7 (pbk.)
    1. Spiders—Juvenile literature. 2. Spiders—North America—Juvenile literature.
[1. Spiders.] I. Title. II. Series.
QL458.4.S68   1999
595.4′4′097—dc21   98-43325
                                                             CIP
                                                             AC

Contents

Is That a Spider?

Everyone knows that spiders eat insects. But wait a minute! Isn't a spider an insect, too? Many people think anything that has lots of legs and crawls around on the ground must be an insect. But that isn't true. A spider is not an insect.

Take a look at the animals pictured on the next page. Which do you think is most closely related to a spider? Which is most distantly related? The answers might surprise you.

A scorpion's huge claws and long, segmented tail make it look more like a lobster than a spider. A horseshoe crab lives in the ocean, and it doesn't look anything like a spider. So the spider's closest relative must be the fly, right?

Wrong! Believe it or not, the scorpion and the horseshoe crab are more closely related to the spider than the fly is. Flies and spiders both belong to a group of animals called *arthropods* [ARH-throh-podz], but that's where the similarity ends. The spider's closest relative is actually the scorpion. The horseshoe crab falls somewhere in between.

Garden spider

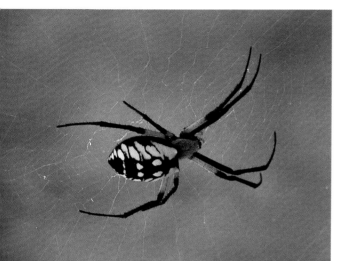

Scorpion

Horseshoe crab

House fly

Traits of a Spider

More than 30,000 different kinds of spiders live in the world. Some are as small as the head of a pin. Others are nearly 4 inches (10 centimeters) long.

Unlike insects, all spiders have a very narrow waist. Their head is fused to their body, so they cannot move it from side to side. All spiders have eight legs covered with bristly hairs. Claws at the tip of each leg grip the surface as a spider walks. Most spiders have eight eyes.

Can you count the eyes of this forest wolf spider?

A Mexican red-knee tarantula with its egg sac

All spiders spin silk, but only some build webs. Spiders that build webs have three claws on each leg. They use their middle claw to cling to the silky strands of their web.

Spiders are meat eaters. A spider's web is a trap built to catch insects and other *prey*. When a helpless insect gets caught in a spider's web, the spider attacks it and pins it down. A spider does not have a stinger, but its jaws can deliver a deadly bite. If you look at a spider's jaws under a magnifying glass, you'll see rows of sharp teeth and two long, curving fangs. There is a tiny hole at the end of each fang. When a spider bites its prey, poison flows out of these holes.

Like many other animals, spiders lay eggs. Most spiders wrap their eggs in tiny sacs made of silk. Although few insects care for their young, some spiders do. When the little *spiderlings* hatch, their mothers feed them until they learn how to hunt for themselves.

The Order of Living Things

A tiger has more in common with a house cat than with a daisy. A true bug is more like a butterfly than a jellyfish. Scientists arrange living things into groups based on how they look and how they act. A tiger and a house cat belong to the same group, but a daisy belongs to a different group.

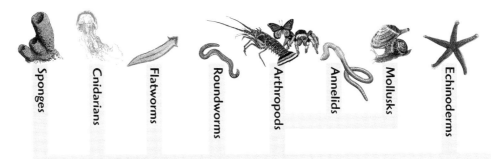

Sponges · Cnidarians · Flatworms · Roundworms · Arthropods · Annelids · Mollusks · Echinoderms

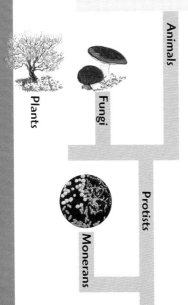

Plants · Fungi · Animals · Protists · Monerans

All living things can be placed in one of five groups called *kingdoms*: the plant kingdom, the animal kingdom, the fungus kingdom, the moneran kingdom, or the protist kingdom. You can probably name many of the creatures in the plant and animal kingdoms. The fungus kingdom includes mushrooms, yeasts, and molds. The moneran and protist kingdoms contain thousands of living things that are too small to see without a microscope.

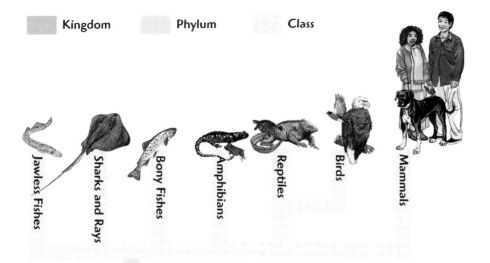

Kingdom Phylum Class

Jawless Fishes

Sharks and Rays

Bony Fishes

Amphibians

Reptiles

Birds

Mammals

Chordates

Because there are millions and millions of living things on Earth, some of the members of one kingdom may not seem all that similar. The animal kingdom includes creatures as different as tarantulas and trout, jellyfish and jaguars, salamanders and sparrows, elephants and earthworms.

To show that an elephant is more like a jaguar than an earthworm, scientists further separate the creatures in each kingdom into more specific groups. The animal kingdom can be divided into nine *phyla*. Humans belong to the chordate phylum. Almost all chordates have a backbone.

Each phylum can be subdivided into many *classes*. Humans, mice, and elephants all belong to the mammal class. Each class can be further divided into *orders*; orders into *families*, families into *genera*, and genera into *species*. All the members of a species are very similar.

How Spiders Fit In

You can probably guess that spiders belong to the animal kingdom. They have much more in common with ticks and turkeys than with maple trees and morning glories.

Spiders belong to the *arthropod* phylum. All arthropods have a tough outer skin. Can you guess what other living things might be arthropods? Examples include scorpions, ladybugs, ticks, and grasshoppers. Many arthropods live in the ocean. Lobsters, crabs, and shrimps all belong to this group.

The arthropod phylum can be divided into a number of different classes. Spiders belong to the *arachnid* [ah-RAK-nid] class. Scorpions, mites, and centipedes are also arachnids. Arachnids have pincers or fangs, but they do not have *antennae*.

There are many different orders of arachnids. The spiders make up one of these orders. Spiders can be divided into a number of different families and genera. These groups can be broken down into about 30,000 different species! Spiders live wherever they can find food. Some live in gardens, around the house, under the ground, in the desert, and even in the water.

All spiders eat other animals. Different species of spiders have different—and sometimes very unusual—ways of capturing prey. As you read the rest of this book, you will learn about spiders that spin webs, spiders that chase or pounce on their prey, spiders that lie in wait underground, and even a spider that spits at its prey!

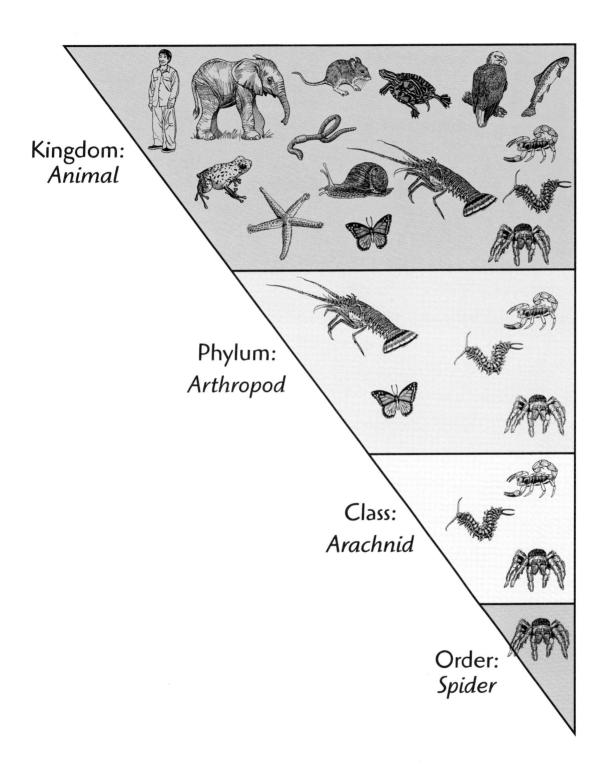

Kingdom:
Animal

Phylum:
Arthropod

Class:
Arachnid

Order:
Spider

Garden Spider

FAMILY: Araneidae
COMMON NAME: Garden spider
GENUS AND SPECIES: *Araneus diadematus*
SIZE: 3/5 inch (1.5 cm)

If you've ever walked through a garden or field on a fall morning, you've probably seen the dew-covered web of a common garden spider. You may have even seen the spider sitting in the center of the web. It was waiting for a fly or a moth to get stuck in its trap.

Garden spiders belong to a group known as orb web spiders. They can build a strong, complex, spiraling web in about an hour. In fact, some garden spiders weave a new web every night. It's easier than repairing old webs that have been damaged by struggling insects.

The hardest step in spinning a web is the first one—stringing the first thread between two objects. To do this, the spider may let a thread blow in the breeze until it catches on something. Sometimes the spider climbs to the ground and back up again, stretching the silk behind it. Then the spider spins threads that run out from the center of the web like the spokes on the wheel of a bicycle. Finally, the spider circles around and around, laying down sticky silk to trap insects.

When the web is finished, the spider waits in the center. If it feels the web shake, the spider knows an insect has flown into the trap. The spider runs across the web, kills the prey with a poisonous bite, and wraps the insect in silk. The spider will eat its meal later.

Money Spider

FAMILY: Linyphiidae
COMMON NAME: Money spider
GENUS AND SPECIES: *Linyphia marginata*
SIZE: 1/16 inch (1.6 mm)

Money spiders build filmy, hammock-like webs. You may have seen these webs covering bushes or small plants in your garden or in the woods. A money spider's web is different from a garden spider's because none of the strands are sticky. Like a real hammock, this spider's web stretches between two points. Sometimes it sags a bit in the center. Other times, the center looks like a dome. That's why some people call these spiders "dome spiders."

After building its web, the money spider hangs upside down underneath it. If an insect lands on the web, it stumbles around clumsily. Try to imagine what it would be like to walk on a hammock.

When the spider feels the web shaking, it scurries across the underside of the web, spears the prey from below, and pulls it down through the web. Later, the spider repairs the holes in its web by laying a new sheet of silk across the torn surface.

Female money spiders lay hundreds of eggs in a single egg sac. When the spiderlings hatch, they climb to the top of a blade of grass, and each one lets out a thin strand of silk. The thread is carried up by the wind, and the little spider is pulled up too. The spiderling may land several hundred feet—or several hundred miles—away. Because the spiderlings spread out over a large area, they do not have to compete for food.

Crab Spider

FAMILY: Thomisidae
COMMON NAME: Crab spider
GENUS AND SPECIES: *Misumena vatia*
SIZE: 2/5 inch (1 cm)

How did the crab spider get its name? It looks like a crab, and it moves like one too. This small spider is usually seen on flowers. It is in constant danger of being eaten by a sharp-eyed bird.

Some crab spiders have solved this problem by blending in with their surroundings. They stay on the petals of flowers that match their body color. Other crab spiders can change color to hide from *predators*. In the summer, these crab spiders are usually white. But when they sit inside a pink rose, they slowly turn pink. Soon after climbing into a yellow daisy, these spiders turn pale gold.

Crab spiders do not build webs. They don't have to. Because they match their surroundings, they are hard to spot as long as they stay perfectly still. As a crab spider lies in wait for an insect, it stretches out its front legs and holds onto the flower with its back legs.

When an insect comes within range, the crab spider grabs the prey with its outstretched legs. Then it sinks its fangs into the back of the insect's head. After a brief struggle, the insect dies.

Wolf Spider

FAMILY: Lycosidae
COMMON NAME: Wolf spider
GENUS AND SPECIES: *Pardosa amentata*
SIZE: 1 inch (2.5 cm)

Have you ever seen a large brown spider resting on a rock or darting across the ground? It was probably a wolf spider. Most wolf spiders live and hunt on the ground. Because they are brown or gray, they blend well with their surroundings.

Wolf spiders are found all over the world, even in the Arctic. These spiders do not wait for insects to come to them. Like real wolves, they chase down their prey. Wolf spiders are very good hunters.

When a wolf spider spots a potential meal, it creeps slowly toward the insect. Then, when it is close enough, the spider darts after its victim and overpowers the helpless creature.

A female wolf spider is an excellent mother. After she lays her eggs, she wraps them in an egg sac made of silk. Then she attaches the sac to her belly and drags it behind her. After several weeks, the female bites a hole in the tough outer covering of the egg sac. Soon, as many as forty tiny spiderlings crawl out and climb onto their mother's back.

For the next few days, the spiderlings all ride piggyback while their mother goes about her daily activities. If a baby falls off, it quickly scurries up one of its mother's eight legs. After about a week, the little spiders jump off and strike out on their own.

Bolas Spider

FAMILY: Araneidae
COMMON NAME: Bolas spider
GENUS AND SPECIES: *Mastophora bisaccata*
SIZE: 3/5 inch (1.5 cm)

The bolas spider has a special way of catching its prey. This fat, wrinkled spider spends its day clinging to a leaf or branch. Its drab color and lumpy shape make it hard to spot.

In the early evening, the bolas spider attaches a single thread to the underside of a twig. While hanging from this thread, it spins a second line about 2 inches (5 cm) long. The spider attaches a ball of very sticky gum to the end of this line, dangles it in the air, and waits.

As it grows dark, moths start to flutter about. Sooner or later, one of them flies within range of the sticky trap. When the spider senses that prey is near, it takes aim and swings its fishing line toward the moth. If the spider hits its target, the moth sticks to the ball like a fly sticks to flypaper. The

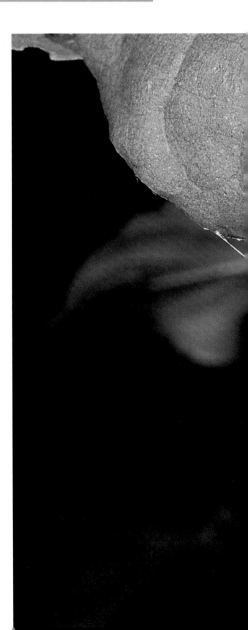

20

spider then reels in the struggling insect and kills it with a deadly bite.

The bolas spider can use the same sticky ball of silk for about 30 minutes before it dries out. When the ball has lost its stickiness, the spider eats it and spins out a new one. A spider may use up several sticky balls before finally catching its dinner.

Zebra Spider

FAMILY: Salticidae
COMMON EXAMPLE: Jumping spider
GENUS AND SPECIES: *Salticus scenicus*
SIZE: Less than 5/8 inch (1.6 cm)

Have you ever seen a little spider basking on a sunny windowsill in your home? If it had four eyes facing forward and four more eyes on top of its head, you were probably looking at a jumping spider.

The jumping spider uses its eyes to find food. Luckily, it has excellent vision. This tiny spider spends its days wandering around in search of flies, beetles, and other small insects. When it spots a likely meal, the spider creeps slowly toward its prey. When it gets close enough, the spider pounces on the unsuspecting insect and delivers its killing bite. Most jumping spiders are very small, but they can leap a long way—up to forty times the length of their body.

The jumping spider's excellent eyesight also comes in handy during the mating season. The males are often brilliantly colored—red, orange, green, or metallic blue. They have long tufts of colored hair on their faces. Needless to say, they are very noticeable—especially to female jumping spiders.

House Spider

FAMILY: Agelenidae
COMMON EXAMPLE: Common house spider
GENUS AND SPECIES: *Tegenaria domestica*
SIZE: 1/2 inch (1.3 cm)

Have you ever been lying in bed at night, and suddenly spotted a big hairy spider crawling up the wall or along the ceiling? If so, you've already met the common house spider. You're more likely to see house spiders in the bathroom though. They often go there to get the water they need to live.

When most people see one of these spiders, their first instinct is to squash it. But there's really nothing to fear. The spider isn't out to get you—it's looking for mosquitoes, flies, and other insects. House spiders eat many of the *pests* that we'd rather not have living with us in the first place.

To catch its prey, the house spider builds a flat, sheet-like web in a corner near the ceiling. Above the sheet is a tangle of silken threads that go up to the ceiling. Have you ever seen someone destroy a cobweb with a broom or suck it into a vacuum cleaner? That web was probably made by a common house spider.

The house spider lives in a little tube at the edge of its web. When an insect flies into the tangle of threads, it falls onto the sheet below. The spider feels the threads shaking, darts out of its tube, and kills the insect.

25

Spitting Spider

FAMILY: *Scytodidae*
COMMON NAME: *Spitting spider*
GENUS AND SPECIES: *Scytodes thoracica*
SIZE: Less than 1/4 inch (6 mm)

You could have spitting spiders in your house and never know it. They are very small. If you ever come across a spitting spider in your basement, in a closet, or in another out-of-the-way place, notice its colorful body. Spitting spiders are light yellow and white with black spots and bands.

You can't blame spitting spiders for any cobwebs you see around the house. They don't build webs. These spiders catch their dinner by spitting at it.

Spitting spiders have special *glands* inside their bodies that make a sticky, gummy substance. When a spitting spider sees a fly or a small moth, it raises its head and squirts two jets of gum through its jaws. At the same time, the spider moves its head quickly from side to side. The gum covers the insect in a zig-zag pattern, and sticks it to the ground. Once the prey is trapped, the spitting spider moves closer to the insect and delivers a deadly bite.

Black Widow Spider

FAMILY: Theridiidae
COMMON NAME: Black widow spider
GENUS AND SPECIES: *Latrodectus mactans*
SIZE: 1/2 inch (1.3 cm)

Do the words "black widow spider" send chills up and down your spine? Most people are afraid of this shiny black spider with a red hourglass-shaped mark on its back.

In reality, the black widow is not a fierce killer. It is shy and spends most of its time alone. This spider may be found in dark places, such as woodpiles, near garbage cans, or in dusty toolsheds. It may bite people if it is caught in clothing, or frightened.

You may have heard that the black widow is one of a few poisonous spiders. That is not true. All spiders inject poison into their prey, but the poison of most spiders is not strong enough to harm people. The black widow's poison can hurt a person. In fact, the black widow's poison is fifteen times more powerful than a rattlesnake's *venom*. If you are bitten by a black widow, you'll feel severe pain. You may also feel dizzy, or you may faint. Luckily, doctors can give you medicine to relieve these symptoms.

Only the female black widow is dangerous. The male is much smaller. He cannot bite or even eat—but he does often get eaten. Did you ever wonder how the black widow got its name? After the spiders mate, the female usually eats the male.

29

Daddy Longlegs

FAMILY: Pholcidae
COMMON NAME: Daddy longlegs
GENUS AND SPECIES: *Pholcus phalangioides*
SIZE: 1/3 inch (8 mm)

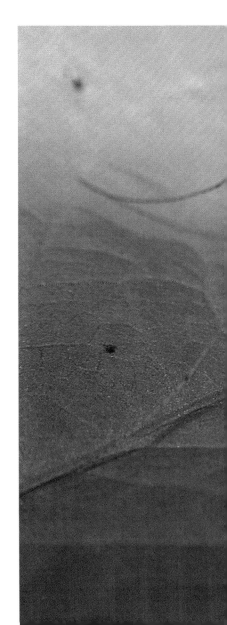

With its long, skinny legs and tiny body, the daddy longlegs is hard to miss. Have you ever seen one hanging upside-down in its large, loosely woven web? Like other house spiders, the daddy longlegs is harmless to people. In fact, it helps us by keeping our homes free of flies and other insects.

Because its legs are so long and thin and its body so small, the daddy longlegs spider is always in danger of drying out. To avoid this, it lives in places that are cool and damp. That's why you are most likely to see one in the bathroom or a dark corner of the basement. If you happen to disturb a daddy longlegs in its web, the spider will shake so much that its entire web starts to move. After a few seconds, its body blends in with its web so well that you can hardly tell which is which. The daddy longlegs uses this trick to confuse enemies.

Many people mistake the daddy longlegs for the harvestman. You may have seen a harvestman outdoors in the late summer or early fall. Although the two creatures look very similar, daddy longlegs and harvestmen are not closely related. In fact, the harvestman is not a spider. It belongs to a different group of arachnids.

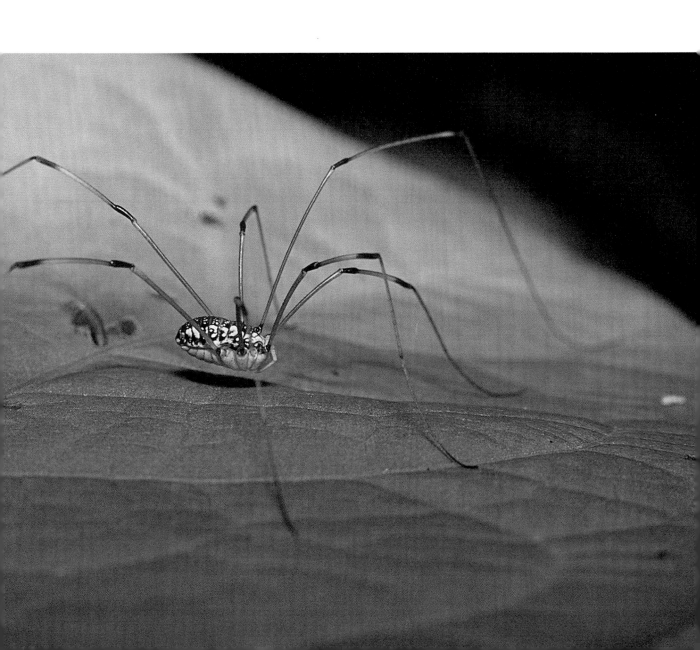

Trapdoor Spider

FAMILY: Ctenizidae
COMMON EXAMPLE: California trapdoor spider
GENUS AND SPECIES: *Bothriocyrtum californicum*
SIZE: 1 inch (2.5 cm)

The trapdoor spider spends its entire life underground. During the day, it rests inside a *burrow* lined with silk. Inside this burrow, the spider is safe from wasps and other enemies.

At night, the spider comes to the top of the burrow, finds a silk door that leads to the surface, and opens it just a crack. When an ant, beetle, or grasshopper passes by, the spider bursts out the door, grabs its prey, and pulls it underground. The attack is over before the helpless insect knows what has happened.

Even though the door to the trapdoor spider's burrow is hidden by leaves and moss, a pompilid wasp may find it. If it does, the spider is in trouble. The wasp will fling open the door, rush into the burrow, and sting the spider.

Sometimes, a trapdoor spider can save itself from this enemy. If the spider senses that a wasp is about to attack, it tries to hold the door closed. Some spiders are extremely strong. The California trapdoor spider can resist an upward pull thirty-seven times its own weight! In the end, though, the wasp usually wins. It can simply cut the door with its powerful jaws.

33

Tarantula

FAMILY: Theraphosidae
COMMON EXAMPLE: Mexican red-knee tarantula
GENUS AND SPECIES: *Brachypelma smithi*
SIZE: 2 inches (5 cm)

Have you ever seen a tarantula in a movie or on TV? Tarantulas are the giants of the spider world. Some species of these large, hairy spiders grow up to 4 inches (10 cm) long and can spread their legs about 11 inches (28 cm).

Like the trapdoor spider, the tarantula is a shy creature. During the day, it hides in underground burrows or under logs or stones. At night, it hunts for food. Small tarantulas eat beetles and other insects. Larger tarantulas may hunt frogs, lizards, and even small snakes.

If a tarantula is attacked by a larger enemy, it has an unusual way of fighting back. Using one of its back legs, the spider rubs off some of the prickly hairs on its belly and throws them in its enemy's face. The sharp hairs may irritate the attacker's skin. If the animal inhales the hairs, it may have trouble breathing. This is enough to send most enemies running in the other direction.

Many years ago, people believed the bite of a European tarantula caused a strange disease. To get well, the sick person had to dance to a certain kind of music. The music and the dance were called the tarantella. That's how the tarantula got its name.

The European tarantula is very poisonous, but the tarantulas that live in North America are no more dangerous than other spiders. If you were bitten by a Mexican red-knee tarantula, it would feel like a sharp pinprick.

Lynx Spider

FAMILY: Oxyopidae
COMMON NAME: Lynx spider
GENUS AND SPECIES: *Peucetia viridans*
SIZE: 3/5 inch (1.5 cm)

Most lynx spiders live on desert plants. They use their excellent eyesight to find prey. When a lynx spider spots an insect, it moves across the plant in quick leaps to catch its dinner. Then it flattens its slender body against a leaf and takes a rest.

The lynx spider is bright green, so it blends well with its surroundings. If it stays perfectly still, it will be safe from most hungry birds.

The female lynx spider is a very good mother. After she lays her eggs, she wraps them in a sac. She guards the large, bulky sac until the spiderlings hatch. Some female lynx spiders lay their eggs among the spines of the prickly pear cactus. Others lay their eggs on one of the stinging plants that grow in desert areas of the southwestern United States. These plants keep the eggs safe from most enemies. After all, what animal wants to get hurt while it's looking for dinner?

Water Spider

FAMILY: Agelenidae
COMMON NAME: Water spider
GENUS AND SPECIES: *Argyroneta aquatica*
SIZE: 1/2 inch (1.3 cm)

Most spiders live on land, but the water spider does not. It spends most of its life underwater.

Like people, spiders must breathe air to stay alive. The water spider has to work hard to make sure it always has enough air. First, the spider spins a small, circular platform and attaches it to an underwater plant. Then it goes to the surface and collects a bubble of air. Holding the bubble between its back legs, the spider dives down to its platform and places the bubble under the circles of silk. It returns to the surface several times to gather more air bubbles.

When the spider has a good supply of air, it crawls inside its air-filled home and sits with its legs dangling. When the spider senses that an insect or tiny fish is near, it darts out of its air bubble, grabs the prey, and tows it inside. The water spider cannot eat its meal in the water. The poison the spider injects will not do its job if it mixes with too much water.

Most male spiders are smaller than the females, but the male water spider is larger than his mate. He builds a platform next to the female's and connects the two with a tube of silk. This makes it easier for the spiders to start an underwater family.

Fun Facts About Spiders

- You probably know that most spiders spin webs, but did you know that the word "spider" comes from an Old English word that means "to spin."

A spider's web

- The first spiders lived close to 300 million years ago. The first flies didn't appear until about 150 million years ago. That means the first spiders had to wait 150 million years for the first flies to turn up in their webs!

A crab spider with a fly

This orb weaver spider is digesting an insect.

- Unlike other animals, spiders *digest* their food before they eat it. Because spiders can swallow only liquids, they inject digestive juices into the bodies of their prey, wait a while, and then suck out the watery mixture.
- Everyone knows that spiders eat insects, but few people realize how many. In Great Britain, the total weight of insects eaten by spiders each year is greater than the total weight of all the people living there.

- As you read earlier, spiders belong to a class of animals called arachnids. This name comes from the story of a young Greek girl named Arachne. Arachne was such a skilled weaver that she challenged the goddess Athena to a weaving contest. When Arachne won, Athena became very angry and destroyed Arachne's work. Arachne was so upset that she killed herself. Athena felt sorry for the girl, so she changed Arachne into a spider.
- Most spiders live just 1 year, but a few live much longer. Female tarantulas sometimes live more than 25 years.

A rose hair tarantula

Words to Know

antenna (plural **antennae**)—a long projection on the head of some animals that is used to sense the world around them

arachnid—the class of animals that includes spiders, scorpions, ticks, and mites

arthropod—the phylum of animals that includes spiders, scorpions, ticks, mites, insects, lobsters, and crabs

burrow—a shelter dug in the ground

class—a group of creatures within a phylum that shares certain characteristics

digest—to break down food

family—a group of creatures within a class that shares certain characteristics

genus (plural **genera**)—a group of creatures within a family that shares certain characteristics

gland—an organ in the body that produces and gives off a liquid

kingdom—one of the five divisions into which all living things are placed: the animal kingdom, the plant kingdom, the fungus kingdom, the moneran kingdom, and the protist kingdom

order—a group of creatures within a class that shares certain characteristics

pest—an animal that is harmful or irritating to humans

phylum (plural **phyla**)—a group of creatures within a kingdom that share certain characteristics

predator—an animal that catches and feeds on other animals

prey—an animal hunted for food by another animal (a predator)

species—a group of creatures within a genus that shares certain characteristics. Members of a species can mate and produce young.

spiderling—a newly hatched spider

venom—a poison that animals use to catch prey or to fight enemies

Learning More

Books

Facklam, Margery and Paul Facklam. *Spiders*. Boston: Little, Brown & Co., 1999.

Robinson, W. Wright. *Spiders, Caterpillars, and Other Silk Makers*. Woodbridge, CT: Blackbirch, 1999.

Ross, Michael Elsohn and Brian Grogan. *Spiderology*. Minneapolis: Carolrhoda Books, 1999.

Web Sites

The American Tarantula Society
http://www.cowboy.net/~spider
This site has the answers to all your questions about tarantulas.

Spider Resources
http://seamonkey.ed.asu.edu/~hixson/index/spiders.html
This site features links to all kinds of sites with information about and photos of spiders.

The Widow Spiders
http://hobospider.org/widows.html
Learn all about the western black widow spider, northern widow spider, red widow spider, brown widow spider, European black widow spider, and the redback spider. This site also describes common symptoms experienced by people bitten by a widow spider.

Index

About the Author

Ann O. Squire, who holds a Ph.D. in animal behavior, has studied a variety of animals, including rats and electric fish. She is the author of several other books on animal behavior, including *101 Questions and Answers About Backyard Wildlife*; *Understanding Man's Best Friend: Why Dogs Look and Act the Way They Do*; and *Anteaters, Sloths, and Armadillos*. This is her second book for Franklin Watts. Dr. Squire lives with her family in Bedford, New York.